RACE
AND SPORTS
MANAGEMENT

BY DUCHESS HARRIS, JD, PHD
WITH MICHAEL MILLER

Essential Library

An Imprint of Abdo Publishing | abdobooks.com

ABDOBOOKS.COM

Published by Abdo Publishing, a division of ABDO, PO Box 398166, Minneapolis, Minnesota 55439. Copyright © 2019 by Abdo Consulting Group, Inc. International copyrights reserved in all countries. No part of this book may be reproduced in any form without written permission from the publisher. Essential Library™ is a trademark and logo of Abdo Publishing.

Printed in the United States of America, North Mankato, Minnesota
092018
012019

THIS BOOK CONTAINS
RECYCLED MATERIALS

Cover Photo: Liu Zishan/Shutterstock Images
Interior Photos: AP Images, 5, 12, 30, 47; Rich Clarkson/Sports Illustrated/Getty Images, 8; RFS/AP Images, 17; Jack Smith/AP Images, 20; Duane Burleson/AP Images, 27; Adrian Wyld/Canadian Press/AP Images, 33; David J. Phillip/AP Images, 37, 86; Amy Sancetta/AP Images, 40; Ron Kuntz Collection/Diamond Images/Getty Images, 49; Lynne Sladky/AP Images, 54; LM Otero/AP Images, 58–59; Larry Goren/Four Seam Images/AP Images, 64; Mark Duncan/AP Images, 69; Patrick Semansky/AP Images, 71; David Banks/AP Images, 74; Charles Rex Arbogast/AP Images, 79; D Dipasupil/Getty Images Entertainment/Getty Images, 81; Darren Abate/AP Images, 82; Stacy Bengs/AP Images, 88; Darron Cummings/AP Images, 89; Michael Conroy/AP Images, 91; Kevin Terrell/AP Images, 93; Tony Gutierrez/AP Images, 98

Editor: Patrick Donnelly
Series Designer: Craig Hinton

LIBRARY OF CONGRESS CONTROL NUMBER: 2018947975

PUBLISHER'S CATALOGING-IN-PUBLICATION DATA

Names: Harris, Duchess, author. | Miller, Michael, author.
Title: Race and sports management / by Duchess Harris and Michael Miller.
Description: Minneapolis, Minnesota : Abdo Publishing, 2019 | Series: Race and sports | Includes online resources and index.
Identifiers: ISBN 9781532116735 (lib. bdg.) | ISBN 9781532159572 (ebook)
Subjects: LCSH: Sports administration--Juvenile literature. | Racism in sports--Juvenile literature. | Race relations--Juvenile literature. | Sports--Juvenile literature.
Classification: DDC 796.089--dc23

CONTENTS

CHAPTER ONE

BREAKING BARRIERS: BILL RUSSELL

It was the seventh and deciding game of the 1969 National Basketball Association (NBA) Finals. The aging Boston Celtics were battling their archrivals, the Los Angeles Lakers. With an average age of 32, the Celtics were thought to be too old to win another NBA championship. The Lakers, boasting a lineup that included future Hall of Famers Elgin Baylor, Jerry West, and Wilt Chamberlain, were the experts' pick to win Game 7 on their home court.

In addition, after a long and storied career, Boston's player-coach Bill Russell was rumored to be retiring after the series. He'd broken the league's color barrier by becoming the NBA's first African American coach three years earlier. And he had led the Celtics—as a player, a coach, or both— to NBA Finals victories over the Lakers in 1959, 1962, 1963, 1965, 1966, and 1968. Now he appeared to be facing his final game as both a player and a coach.

The Lakers were confident that this was the year they'd finally beat the Celtics. Before the game, their team owner ordered thousands of purple and gold balloons suspended from the rafters, and on every seat a flyer was placed that read, "When the Lakers win the championship, the USC marching band will play 'Happy Days Are Here Again.' Balloons will fall down."

This served only to inspire the Celtics. Before the game, Russell told his players, "One thing cannot happen, the Lakers cannot beat us. It's not something that can happen. But it will be fun watching the Lakers get those balloons down one at a time."[1]

It was all the motivation the Celtics needed. Boston took an early 24–12 advantage, then held off a Lakers charge for a 59–56 halftime lead. In the second half, Russell's defensive play controlled the Lakers' scoring while the Celtics ran up a 79–66 lead in the third quarter. That lead grew to 17 points early in the fourth quarter, but then the Lakers, led by West's hot shooting, cut the lead to one point with three minutes

Russell is mobbed by University of San Francisco fans after he led the Dons to victory in the 1955 NCAA title game.

to go. With the game and the title on the line, Russell and the Celtics' defense kept the Lakers at bay, and Boston took home the NBA title with a 108–106 final.

In three years as Boston's player-coach, Russell had won two more NBA titles. That ran his overall total to 11 in his 13 years with the Celtics. It had been rough going at times, but he showed that an African American could successfully run a team at the highest level of sports.

GROWING UP POOR AND BLACK

William Felton Russell was born on February 12, 1934, in the small town of West Monroe, Louisiana. Bill's grandfather,

Jake, had been a sharecropper, a farmer who rented small plots of land from white landowners in return for a meager portion of the crops. Bill's father, Charlie, worked as a janitor in a local paper mill. It was a life not far removed from slavery; in fact, Bill's father knew older men and women who had been enslaved when they were younger.

Bill himself grew up in an era in which black people weren't allowed to shop at white-owned stores or use white-only restrooms and swimming pools. After Bill's mother, Katie, was threatened with arrest by a policeman for wearing a dress that he thought was "white women's clothing," Bill's father decided to move his family to California, where he hoped to find more opportunity and less overt prejudice.

For young Bill, the move from the segregated South was a blessing. He was amazed that, in California, there weren't separate black and white drinking fountains as there were in the South. Bill attended integrated schools, made both black and white friends, and became interested in sports— track and field at first, then basketball.

PLAYING BALL

Bill lacked basic basketball skills and struggled as a player throughout his high school years. He was offered just one scholarship, to the nearby University of San Francisco (USF). At USF, Bill worked on his fundamentals and developed a

USF BREAKS THROUGH

African American players did not have many opportunities to participate in sports at major colleges and universities before the 1950s. The 1954–55 USF team made history by being the first team to include three African Americans—Bill Russell, K. C. Jones, and Hal Perry—in the starting lineup. As a team, they ran into the segregation that was common at the time, often being refused service at restaurants and hotels.

new and unique approach to defensive play, running and jumping to block shots in a way that was in direct contrast with the less aggressive defense common at the time. Bill's innovative defense led the USF Dons to a string of 55 consecutive victories and two National Collegiate Athletic Association (NCAA) championships. He then joined the US basketball team that won gold at the 1956 Summer Olympics in Melbourne, Australia.

Russell was the second pick in the 1956 NBA draft, chosen by the Saint Louis Hawks and immediately traded to the Celtics. This was part of a plan by Boston general manager and coach Arnold "Red" Auerbach to build what would become a basketball dynasty. The league hadn't been integrated long; Auerbach had drafted the NBA's first black player, Chuck Cooper, in 1950. In fact, only 15 black players were on NBA rosters the year Russell joined.[3]

At six feet ten inches (208 cm) tall, Russell wasn't the biggest or most physical center in the league, but he may have been the smartest. He was able to anticipate the moves of his opponents, blocking their shots, grabbing key rebounds, and changing the flow of the game. Russell's presence made a difference; the Celtics finished the year with a 44–28 record, their best in four years, and then went on to win their first NBA championship.

That was just the start of the Celtics' dynasty. During his first ten years in Boston, Russell led the team to nine league titles and was named NBA Most Valuable Player (MVP) five times. It was indeed the era of Bill Russell and the Boston Celtics.

TEXAS WESTERN SHOCKS KENTUCKY

The case for integration took a major step forward in 1966 when Texas Western University became the first college basketball team to start five black players in the NCAA championship game. Texas Western defeated Kentucky—an all-white team from the heavily segregated South—to win the title.

BECOMING THE FIRST BLACK COACH

Following Russell's tenth season with the Celtics, Auerbach retired as head coach but remained as the team's general manager. He chose Russell, the Celtics' captain, as his successor. When Russell accepted the title of player-coach on April 16, 1966, he became the first African American head coach not only in the NBA but in any major league professional sports team.

Red Auerbach, right, *trusted Russell to take over the Celtics' coaching duties in 1966.*

When asked whether Auerbach had chosen him because of his race, Russell said, "I wasn't offered the job because I am a Negro, I was offered it because Red figured I could do it."[4] Auerbach was right: Russell could do it. The basketball smarts and team-building skills that had made him such a formidable player also made him a successful coach.

It wouldn't be easy, on or off the court. As sports columnist Claude E. Harrison Jr. of the *Philadelphia Tribune* put it, Russell "is the first Negro to head a major sports team and the eyes of the world will be upon him, some wishing him well and others wishing him ill."[5]

Russell had to deal not just with being the coach but also with being an active player. When asked on the first day of training camp what he might think about in the closing moments of a game, Russell responded, "I figured there'd be three things to do. To play, to try to substitute, and to figure strategy. And I've had a tough enough time playing!"[6]

Russell also brought his formidable team-building skills to his new job as coach. Throughout his playing career he had focused on supporting the other players, not himself. As Russell put it, "The most important measure of how good a game I played was how much better I made my teammates play."[7] During his tenure as coach, Russell continued with this team-first approach. He took a mix of aging and newer players and molded them into a team that continued to dominate a younger, more athletic league.

The simmering racial tensions of the time made Russell's job more difficult. While black players were rare, a black coach was unheard of. At the press conference announcing his appointment as head coach, one reporter insultingly asked whether Russell would be able to coach without discriminating against the team's white players. Russell himself received numerous insults and threatening letters. When he bought a home in a predominantly white area of Boston, vandals broke into his house, painted the walls with racist graffiti, and defecated on his bed. On the court, he endured taunts from racist fans in Boston and elsewhere.[8]

A CIVIL RIGHTS ADVOCATE

Perhaps because of his firsthand experiences with racial prejudice, Russell became one of the greatest and most outspoken civil rights advocates in American sports. He participated in the historic March on Washington in August 1963 and heard Dr. Martin Luther King Jr.'s famous "I Have a Dream" speech. He supported Muhammad Ali when the boxer refused to serve in the military due to his religious beliefs. He used his celebrity to draw attention to the civil rights movement.

Russell pushed for equality and was not afraid of speaking his mind on that or any other subject. That didn't always make him popular in the league or in Boston. But Russell's efforts were acknowledged in 2011, when President Barack Obama awarded him the Presidential Medal of Freedom, the highest honor possible for any American outside of the military.

Occasionally, he and his black teammates were refused service in restaurants.

Still, Russell stayed focused on his job and on his team. Although the Celtics didn't win a championship during his first year as player-coach, they were league champions the following two years—bringing Russell's lifetime record to 11 NBA championships.

Russell retired from the Celtics following the 1968–69 season. He coached for two more teams (the Seattle SuperSonics and Sacramento Kings) before retiring for good in 1988. The Celtics went on to have several African American coaches over the years, including Russell's former teammate K. C. Jones.

A REMARKABLE LEGACY

Few players or coaches have had the impact that Bill Russell had on the game of basketball and on professional sports in general. In addition to his significant contributions as a player, Russell broke the color barrier in the ranks of professional coaching; before Russell, it would have been unheard of to even consider a black man for a job as head coach of a major league sports team.

Russell accomplished all this while also experiencing the racial prejudice of his time—a prejudice that endures, in lesser degrees, to this day. Because of his innate personal skills, his tenacity, and the goodwill he earned from his teammates, Russell proved his worth to a skeptical audience. His success as the first African American NBA coach thus paved the way for dozens of other African Americans to earn coaching positions in major professional and college sports.

DISCUSSION STARTERS

- How would you have handled the prejudice Bill Russell encountered as a black basketball player in the 1950s and 1960s?
- How do you think race factored into Red Auerbach's decision to promote Bill Russell to head coach of the Boston Celtics?
- Do you think Bill Russell would have encountered the same prejudices if he had coached for a team in another part of the country?

CHAPTER TWO

WHY DIVERSITY MATTERS

D iversity is a word that can mean different things to different people. In general, diversity means including different types of people in a group or organization. In the sports world, diversity involves recruiting athletes of different races and cultures, as well as hiring them to coach and including them in team and league management.

Today's sports world is much more diverse than it used to be. Through the 1960s, professional and major college sports reflected the racial divides that defined American society at the time. The fans were primarily white, most of the players were white, and the coaches, team management, and owners were white, as well.

That changed over time, much as the country's attitudes toward race changed when the civil rights movement sought to desegregate American society. The player ranks were integrated first, with three modern professional sports leagues—the NBA, the National Football League (NFL), and Major League Baseball (MLB)—signing their first nonwhite players by 1950. It took longer for major league teams to hire minority head coaches.

MANAGEMENT DIVERSITY

It took decades for people of color to fully integrate major league coaching and management staffs. Russell became the first black NBA coach in 1966. The Cleveland Indians made Frank Robinson the first African American MLB manager in October 1974. And it took until 1989 before the Los Angeles Raiders hired Art Shell as the modern NFL's first African American head coach.

Even today there is a notable lack of diversity in team management positions—presidents, general managers,

DODGER DISGRACE

Al Campanis, a former Los Angeles Dodgers executive, was Jackie Robinson's roommate and teammate when the two played minor league baseball in Montreal in 1946. After retiring, Campanis moved up the ranks in the Dodgers' front office, serving as a scout, scouting director, general manager, and eventually vice president for player personnel. Along the way, the Dodgers developed a reputation as one of the most forward-thinking, diverse organizations in all of sports.

That's why it came as such a shock when Campanis torpedoed his career and tarnished his legacy with racially charged comments in a 1987 episode of the ABC TV show *Nightline*. Campanis appeared as a guest during a segment devoted to celebrating the fortieth anniversary of Robinson's debut with the Brooklyn Dodgers. When host Ted Koppel asked him why there wasn't more diversity off the field in MLB organizations, Campanis said that black people "may not have some of the necessities to be a field manager or general manager" in professional baseball.[1] He was forced to resign two days later after the Dodgers said they wouldn't accept such backward thinking in their organization.

In 1989, the Raiders' Art Shell became the first black head coach in modern NFL history.

and ownership. Some blame racial stereotyping, including the mistaken prejudice that black people and other minorities are intellectually inferior to whites and thus not qualified for coaching and management roles. Others blame the so-called old-boys network—the thought that mostly white, mostly male executives typically hire people whom they already know rather than stretch beyond their usual list of contacts when searching for job candidates. Social relationships play an important role in any hiring situation,

MINORITY REPRESENTATION IN PROFESSIONAL SPORTS[2]

	PLAYERS	HEAD COACH/ MANAGER	PRESIDENT/ CEO	GENERAL MANAGER	SENIOR ADMINISTRATOR	OWNER
MLB (2018)	42.5%	13.3%	0%	13.3%	20.0%	2.5%
NBA (2017–18)	80.7%	30.0%	9.8%	20.0%	31.2%	10.0%
NFL (2018)	72.6%	25.0%	0%	18.8%	18.2%	6.2%

SOURCE: INSTITUTE FOR DIVERSITY AND ETHICS IN SPORT

especially in sports. In the predominantly white world of professional sports, this makes it difficult for people of color (as well as women and younger candidates) to break into the ranks.

Many experts believe the percentage of minority coaches and team management should mirror the percentage of nonwhite players in each league. However, that is not the case; the percentage of nonwhite coaches and management is at best one-third of the percentage of minority players.

At the team ownership level, diversity barely exists. Out of 30 NBA teams, only three have people of color who are majority owners. That number is even lower in the NFL (two of 32 teams) and in MLB (one of 30 teams).

More diverse ownership and team management can help attract better people for all positions, including the coaching staff. When a team casts a wider net for a given position, it's more likely to find a superior candidate. N. Jeremi Duru, author of *Advancing the Ball: Race, Reformation, and the Quest for Equal Coaching Opportunity in the NFL*, points out this benefit of diverse recruiting: "It's the idea that in order to succeed and be competitive, you have to look at a deep pool of candidates. . . . The idea is that it really becomes clear that the best coaches come from all sorts of different places."[3]

DIVERSE MANAGEMENT AFFECTS TEAM DYNAMICS

But diversity isn't just important in sports; it can strengthen any organization. The unique experiences and viewpoints brought by people from different backgrounds can help break through stale thinking and introduce new ideas and ways of doing things. Instead of always doing things the same old way, diverse contributors help a team adopt new approaches and keep up with changing trends.

Players also need to connect with the people coaching and managing them. That's an argument for hiring a coaching staff that mirrors the diversity of a team's roster. Steve Williams, the director of pro scouting for the Pittsburgh Pirates and president of the Buck O'Neil

Professional Baseball Scouts & Coaches Association, spoke of this issue:

> *All players like to see people that look like them, whether you're Latin, white, African American, Japanese, whatever. They want to have someone that they can dialogue with, that understands what they're going through. When you only see it from one side, you don't totally understand what some of the players are going through.*[4]

Minority coaches often can better relate to and manage minority players. A young African American player may

FAN-FRIENDLY PLANS

Several marketing directors interviewed for an NCAA study noted that due to increasing ticket prices, families with lower incomes simply couldn't afford to attend many games. As a result, many of these directors developed lower-priced multigame ticket plans directly targeted at minority families. In one instance, a team's marketing department developed a "family four pack," which included four game tickets, four hot dogs, and four drinks for a bargain price. The study noted that this school's results were impressive, with sales increasing from 200 plans sold in the promotion's first year to 1,000 sold in year three.

Enticing more people of color into the stands also puts pressure on teams to further diversify management and coaching staff. One of the reasons teams could discriminate in the past was that people of color were not their primary consumers; the more nonwhite fans teams attract, the more they need to listen to those fans when making hiring decisions.

be reluctant to take advice given by an older white coach but might develop a better relationship with a coach of the same color and background. This holds true for foreign-born players, who may better identify with a coach who speaks their native language. This can result in a better attitude, more consistent performance, and improved teamwork from players of color, which translates into results on the field or court. As one minority NFL coach told an ESPN reporter, "You'd better have some guys who can relate to the black players on the team or you are going to have a hard time."[5]

DIVERSITY ATTRACTS FANS

Studies have shown that diversity within a sports administration can attract more and more diverse fans.

REFLECTING COMMUNITY DEMOGRAPHICS

Some experts argue that it is misguided to expect the number of minority coaches and front office staff to track with the large number of people of color playing the game. Instead, they say, the percentage of minorities in coaching and management should reflect the racial makeup of society as a whole. Looking at 2017 US Census estimates, approximately 18 percent of Americans are Hispanic, 13 percent are black, 6 percent are Asian, and 1.3 percent are Indigenous people.[6] Compared with these overall numbers, one would expect approximately 37 percent of coaching and management positions to be filled by nonwhites. Yet even by this measurement, coaching and management diversity lag far behind the country's racial demographics.

An NCAA analysis of 258 Division I college athletics departments found that schools that value diversity tend to have more success reaching a diverse fan base.[7] A more diverse management group has a better chance of understanding the team's marketplace. Put another way, if a team's front office doesn't understand or relate to the culture of the team's fan base, it can't effectively market to them. Hiring staff who mirror the ethnicity of fans makes for a stronger connection.

In short, a commitment to diversity offers countless advantages at every level of an organization. But it took a long time for the sports world to catch on.

DISCUSSION STARTERS

- Do you think the coaching and management ranks of a major sports league should reflect the racial makeup of the league's players or of a team's surrounding community? Why?
- Why do you think diversity levels differ from sport to sport?
- As a fan, does it matter to you whether a team has a nonwhite coach or diverse management staff?

CHAPTER THREE

RISING THROUGH THE NBA RANKS

In the 50 years after Bill Russell became the first black head coach in the NBA, 68 other black men were given opportunities to be NBA head coaches. Some lasted less than a single season, while some won NBA championships. All of them brought their own unique perspectives to the game and helped the NBA become the most diverse league in professional sports today.

When one examines the most successful black coaches in the NBA, the name "Doc" is near the top of everybody's list. Glenn Anton "Doc" Rivers is not only one of the most successful black coaches in the NBA today. He's one of the most successful coaches in league history.

Like most head coaches in any sport, Rivers started out as a player. He spent 13 years as an NBA point guard before being hired as the Orlando Magic's head coach in 1999. In his first year with the Magic, Rivers took home NBA Coach of the Year honors—a rare accomplishment for a rookie coach.

Rivers stayed in Orlando until 2004, when he moved to Boston. There he led the Celtics to an NBA championship in 2008. In 2013, he joined the Los Angeles Clippers, where he also served as president of basketball operations. That made him one of the few African Americans in NBA senior management. Through 2018, Rivers had won nearly 850 games, ranking him in the top 15 of the career victory list for NBA head coaches.

BLACK COACHES JOIN THE LEAGUE

After Russell became the first black NBA coach in 1966, it took only a few years for other African American coaches to follow in his footsteps. The year after Russell retired from the Celtics, Lenny Wilkens became the league's second black coach when he took over the Seattle SuperSonics for the 1969–70 season. Al Attles became the third black coach in the league when he coached a partial season for the San Francisco Warriors that same year.

Minority coaches bring their own unique perspectives to the coaching game and also serve as important role models.

Lenny Wilkens, left, the second black head coach in NBA history, led the Seattle SuperSonics to the league title in 1979.

African American kids playing the game in elementary, middle, and high school can look up to and learn from the many black coaches in the NBA—role models who look like them and are succeeding in the big leagues.

FROM PLAYER TO COACH

When it comes to rookie coaches, a large number are former players—especially in the ranks of African American coaches. Of the seven black NBA coaches in 2015, five (71 percent) were former NBA players. Of that season's white

WHERE NBA COACHES COME FROM

Where do NBA teams find their head coaches? In the 2017–18 season, the league's top teams demonstrated several different approaches to finding a head coach.

Many teams hire veteran coaches from elsewhere in the league; it's not unusual for an experienced coach to serve three or more teams over the course of an NBA career. In 2017–18, Houston Rockets head coach Mike D'Antoni coached his fifth NBA team over his 20-year coaching career, leading the Rockets to the No. 1 seed in the Western Conference.

There is also a growing trend toward hiring coaches from the college ranks. Brad Stevens jumped directly from Butler University to the Boston Celtics head coaching job at age 37 in 2013. Four seasons later, he led the Celtics to the second-best record in the Eastern Conference.

Finally, many head coaches, especially black coaches, are recently retired players. Tyronn Lue led the Cleveland Cavaliers to the NBA Finals three years in a row after taking over as head coach midway through the 2015–16 season. Lue spent 11 years as an NBA player and three and a half more as an assistant coach before getting the Cavaliers' top job.

coaches, however, only eight (36 percent) had significant NBA playing careers.[2]

Dr. Todd Boyd, a professor of race and popular culture at the University of Southern California, notes that while white coaches have multiple avenues into the league, black coaches enter almost exclusively via the player route—which could limit the number of African American coaching candidates.

"If you go around the NBA," Boyd notes, "you can find a lot of white people working in various positions who never played in the NBA. Almost every black person you find within the NBA . . . the majority of those people played in the NBA."[3]

One example of that trend is Mark Jackson, a popular point guard who played for seven NBA teams from 1987 to 2004, including the New York Knicks and the Indiana Pacers. After retiring as a player, he spent several years announcing NBA games on cable television. In 2011, he was hired as head coach for the Golden State Warriors despite having no prior coaching experience. During his three years there, he led the Warriors to their first 50-win season in almost 20 years, as well as two consecutive playoff appearances.

HELD TO A HIGHER STANDARD

While there are more black coaches today than there were in previous decades, they seem to be held to a higher standard than their white counterparts. Many coaches of color have lost their jobs after achieving successes for their teams that other coaches—most of whom were white—did not match.

For example, when the Warriors fired Jackson in 2014, he had just led the team to back-to-back playoff appearances for the first time since 1992. Similarly, the Toronto Raptors fired Sam Mitchell in 2008, one year after he had coached the Raptors to their most wins in team history and been named the 2007 NBA Coach of the Year.

Surrounded by his Toronto Raptors players, Sam Mitchell receives the 2007 NBA Coach of the Year Award.

Would these coaches have retained their positions if they were white? Warriors owner Joe Lacob says Jackson was fired because he didn't get along with the rest of the organization and didn't hire a strong enough staff. Mitchell was fired after a disappointing start to a new season; some critics say that despite his past record, he had a poor grasp of fundamentals and wasn't building a strong bench.

These are all valid reasons for which teams might want to change coaches. But some observers question whether this is part of a pattern that sets the bar higher for minority coaches than for white coaches. The criticisms these coaches faced rely on factors that are difficult to quantify and are thus difficult to disprove. And they carry with them a sour hint of traditional negative stereotypes against successful black athletes— arrogant, not intelligent, not a team player.

Commenting on Jackson's firing, journalist Noah Gulliver noted that black coaches "are held up to impossibly high standards. Mark Jackson is just the latest example. . . . Those of us who can see the truth can see that Mark Jackson didn't get a fair shake—and we know why that is."[5]

Backing up that claim, data shows that black coaches in the NBA have shorter tenures than their white counterparts. Over the ten-season period from 2005–06 to 2014–15, black coaches lasted just 2.85 seasons on average, compared with white coaches' average of 3.2 seasons. That's a 12 percent or 29-game gap, which provides white coaches a longer period to prove themselves in their positions.[6]

Some people believe that black coaches remain victims of old stereotypes about athletes and intelligence. As Boyd notes, "I think there's this perception, perhaps unconscious and perhaps unspoken, that a lot of black guys just aren't smart enough to do the job."[7]

DISCUSSION STARTERS

- Why do you think black NBA coaches come primarily from the player ranks and not from other coaching or assistant positions?
- Do you think minority NBA coaches are given the same opportunities to succeed as their white peers? Why or why not?
- What do you think the NBA could do to attract more black coaches and help them become successful?

CHAPTER FOUR

GRIDIRON GUIDANCE

Mike Tomlin led the Pittsburgh Steelers to a Super Bowl victory in just his second year as head coach.

T he NFL was the first major American sports league to integrate minority players. The first African American player to play in the modern era in the NFL was running back Kenny Washington, who joined the Los Angeles Rams in 1946. By the 2017 season, 73 percent of NFL players were black.[1]

It took a lot longer for the NFL to integrate its coaching ranks. After the Raiders hired Art Shell in 1989, just 19 other black head coaches were hired through 2018. In the 2018 season, there were eight minority coaches (seven black, one Hispanic) among the NFL's 32 teams—25 percent of the total.

Minority coaches, though late to the game, have seen success. More than half of these nonwhite coaches have led their teams to ten or more wins in a season. Two African American coaches, Tony Dungy and Mike Tomlin, have won Super Bowls. In addition, Hispanic coach Tom Flores won two Super Bowls with the Los Angeles Raiders.[2]

All of this is in defiance of long-standing thinking that black and other minorities weren't smart enough to coach in the NFL.

INTEGRATING THE NFL

Black players were an accepted part of the NFL at its inception in 1920. In its early years, the league had several black players on team rosters. In fact, the first black coach in NFL history came in this era, when Fritz Pollard was named co-coach for the Akron Pros in 1921.

This acceptance of African American players in the league changed in 1933, when Boston Braves owner George Preston Marshall forced the NFL to institute an informal ban on black players and coaches. Marshall, a notorious racist, also was the man responsible for renaming his club the Redskins, a name that remains controversial today for the team, which now plays in Washington, DC.

The NFL's unspoken ban on black players stayed in effect for more than a decade. Then, in 1946, a new competitor to the NFL, the All-America Football Conference, began signing talented black players, signaling the integration that was on the horizon for all major sports in the United States.

Also that year, the NFL's Cleveland Rams moved to Los Angeles. They wanted to play their home games in the Los Angeles Memorial Coliseum, but African American newspapers voiced their objections to allowing a segregated league to play in a municipal stadium. The Rams relented and signed former University of California, Los Angeles (UCLA), star running back Kenny Washington, integrating the modern NFL. Marshall's Redskins became the final team to sign a black player in 1962.

THE MYTH ABOUT BLACK INTELLIGENCE

For a long time, the NFL labored under the harmful myth that while black people were well suited for brute-force positions on the field, they lacked the intelligence to handle jobs that required more brainpower. This myth led many to believe that a black man could be a linebacker or a wide receiver or even a running back, but he simply wasn't smart enough to call plays as a quarterback. This myth carried

Tony Dungy was the first black head coach to win a Super Bowl, leading the Indianapolis Colts to the title after the 2006 season.

over to coaching. Team owners believed the stereotype that only white people had the intellectual know-how to cut it as head coaches. Maybe a black coach could handle working with one position, such as wide receivers or defensive linemen, but they weren't smart enough to come up with sophisticated plays. This backward thinking influenced whom owners hired for that position. Many also didn't think their fan base would support a black coach.

Regarding the lack of black head coaches, writer Louis Moore said, "[It] signaled two things. One, owners did not believe black people had the intellect or fortified character to lead white men. Two, owners spent too much time worrying about how white fans would react."[3]

Even after Shell took the head coaching position for the Raiders in 1989, only three more African Americans were hired as coaches over the next decade. It took until the 2000s—and the implementation of a new league rule—for African Americans to truly break into the NFL's coaching ranks.

THE ROONEY RULE CHANGES THE GAME

At the start of the 2001 season, the NFL had three black head coaches: Tony Dungy (Tampa Bay Buccaneers), Herm Edwards (New York Jets), and Dennis Green (Minnesota Vikings). By the end of that season, two of those coaches (Dungy and Green) had been fired—seemingly without good reason. Green had been a head coach for ten years and just had his first losing season; Dungy had a winning record the year he was fired.

In late October 2002, inspired by these firings, two civil rights lawyers sent a letter to the NFL, seeking more head coaching opportunities for African Americans. The letter referenced a report they had developed, called *Black Coaches in the National Football League: Superior*

Performance, Inferior Opportunities. The report noted that African American coaches in the NFL were typically the last hired and the first fired, despite having superior win-loss records. It also noted that too few African Americans were offered interviews by teams seeking to fill the head coaching position.

In response to this study, the NFL put together a group of minority coaches, scouts, and front office personnel to examine the situation. This group, headed by Dan Rooney, former owner of the Pittsburgh Steelers and chair of the NFL's diversity committee, lobbied for more minority representation in the coaching ranks.

In 2003, after much debate, the NFL instituted the Rooney Rule to directly address the diversity issue. The way the Rooney Rule works is simple: when an NFL team has an opening for a head coaching position, it is

EXPANDING THE ROONEY RULE

In recent years, the NFL has taken steps to make the Rooney Rule even more effective. In 2009, the rule was expanded to include general manager and equivalent front office positions. In addition, the league created a career development symposium at Wharton School of Business for potential minority coaches, where they can learn from current NFL owners, general managers, and coaches. The league also formed an advisory panel of former general managers and head coaches, charged with producing a short list of potential minority candidates for coaching and general management positions each year.

required to interview at least one minority candidate before that position is filled.

The rule does not dictate that a team must hire a certain percentage of minorities, only that at least one minority candidate must be considered for any open position. If a team does *not* interview a minority candidate, it is fined for that offense. This happened in 2003, shortly after the rule was put into place, when the Detroit Lions hired Steve Mariucci, a white coach, without interviewing any minority candidates. The team had to pay a $200,000 fine.

Has the Rooney Rule worked as intended? The answer is an unqualified yes. In the 12 years before the Rooney Rule, the league had only six total nonwhite head coaches. In the

TONY DUNGY: IMPROVING DIVERSITY

Tony Dungy is one of the most important faces of diversity in the NFL's history. Not only is he one of the reasons the NFL enacted the Rooney Rule but he also had tremendous success with the two teams he coached—the Tampa Bay Buccaneers (1996–2001) and the Indianapolis Colts (2002–2008). He became the first black coach to win the Super Bowl when he led the Colts to the title after the 2006 season.

Dungy was also responsible for hiring a large number of promising assistant coaches, including many minorities. Seven of Dungy's former assistants went on to become head coaches for other teams; five of the seven were minorities. Dungy's staff accounted for 33 percent of the minority head-coaching hires in the two decades after he joined the league, including 29 percent of those hired since the Rooney Rule took effect.[4] Dungy has identified and mentored more minority talent than any other person or team in the league's history.

12 years after the Rooney Rule was enacted, another 14 minority head coaches were hired.[5]

DIVERSITY IN THE POST-ROONEY ERA

Even with the Rooney Rule in place, the hiring of minority coaches appears to have plateaued in recent years. Teams have been accused of going through the motions with a token interview of a minority candidate before hiring the white coach they wanted all along. The teams, on the other hand, blame the problem on not having enough qualified minority candidates among the ranks of top NFL assistants, from which they promote the majority of their head coaches.

The problem is made worse by the league's tendency to promote more offensive coordinators than defensive coordinators to head coaches. Of the 99 full-time NFL head coaching jobs filled between 2007 and 2017, more than half (52) had primarily offensive backgrounds, but only five of those men (10 percent) were black. Of the 46 head coaches with primarily defensive backgrounds, 13 (28 percent) were black.[6] (One head coach—John Harbaugh of the Baltimore Ravens—was a former special teams coordinator.)

This may play to the myth of inferior black intelligence. Offensive coordinators are often former quarterbacks, a position that requires a higher "football IQ" and thus has traditionally been stocked with a disproportionate number of white players. Meanwhile, the ideal defensive coordinator is thought to be someone who is more a leader and a motivator than a thinker. As one anonymous black offensive coach said, "Being a defensive coach is not considered a thinking man's job. It's about reaction and emotion. Nobody wants to hire a black coach because of his mind."[7]

Put simply, NFL teams are less likely to hire people of color as offensive coordinators than they are as defensive coordinators—and they are more likely to promote offensive coordinators to become head coach than defensive coordinators. To alleviate this issue, many believe that the Rooney Rule should be expanded to include coordinator and other assistant positions. This would promote more diversity throughout the entire coaching staff.

DISCUSSION STARTERS

- Why do you think it took the NFL so much longer than the NBA to embrace minority head coaches?
- Do you think the Rooney Rule goes far enough to bring people of color into the coaching ranks?
- Why do you think the number of minority coaches appears to have plateaued in the NFL?

CHAPTER FIVE

FROM THE DIAMOND TO THE DUGOUT

Professional baseball was one of the first sports to integrate minority players into the game. Jackie Robinson famously became the first black player in the modern-day major leagues when he joined the Brooklyn Dodgers on April 15, 1947. He was quickly followed by other black players—but no black managers.

Twenty-five years after Robinson broke the league's color barrier, he was invited to throw out the ceremonial first pitch at Game 2 of the 1972 World Series. Speaking before 53,224 fans, he used the occasion to comment on the lack of black managers in the sport.

"I am extremely proud and pleased to be here this afternoon," Robinson said, "but must admit, I am going to be tremendously more pleased and more proud when I look at that third-base coaching line one day and see a black face managing in baseball."[1]

That didn't happen until October 1974, when the Cleveland Indians hired Frank Robinson (no relation to Jackie) to be baseball's first black manager. There have been more nonwhite managers since then, but not many, which raises the question: With so many African American and Latino players in the league, why are minorities so underrepresented among the ranks of managers?

Frank Robinson meets with the media after guiding the Indians to victory over the New York Yankees in his first game as manager.

BASEBALL HAS A DIVERSITY PROBLEM

Unlike professional basketball and football, where roughly three-quarters of all players are nonwhite, the percentage of minorities playing Major League Baseball more closely reflects the demographics of overall American society. Comparing diversity numbers in 2017, approximately 43 percent of MLB players were nonwhite, which roughly mirrored the percentage of nonwhites in the general population (37 percent).

WHY THE DECLINE IN BLACK PLAYERS?

One reason for the decline in black MLB players is the lack of diversity in college baseball, where less than 5 percent of Division I players are African American.[4] It also reflects the lack of opportunities for black youth to play the game; equipment is expensive, and baseball fields are few and far between in crowded inner cities and suburbs.

It hasn't always been this way. Baseball once was a game kids could play in their neighborhoods. Pickup games formed in vacant lots throughout cities, suburbs, and small towns. As the country grew and the demand for housing increased, those lots were paved over or filled with houses. These days, kids who want to play baseball usually have to pay entry fees to join a team in a league run by adults. It's more organized now, and it's also more expensive. Upper- and middle-class kids have more access to these organized leagues than do most minority youth. This explains, to some extent, why poorer and minority kids have gravitated to basketball and soccer, sports that don't require money, adults, or a dedicated field to play.

Of these players of color, African Americans were underrepresented at about 8 percent of the players versus 13 percent of the general population. Latinos, on the other hand, were significantly overrepresented, at 32 percent of MLB players versus 17 percent of the US population.[2] This is a significant change over the past two decades. In 1991, 17 percent of MLB players were African American, while just 16 percent were Latino.[3] While the total minority representation has actually increased over that time frame (33 percent in 1991 versus 43 percent in 2017), that's a big decline in the percentage of black players—and a big increase in Latinos.

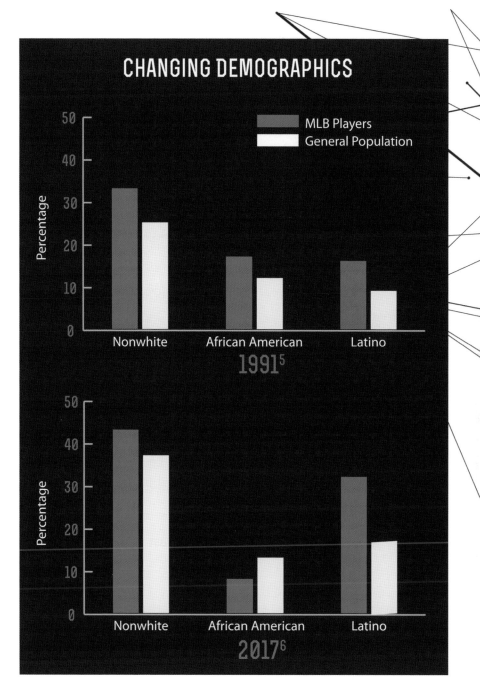

CHANGING DEMOGRAPHICS

1991[5]

2017[6]

Legend: MLB Players / General Population

Categories: Nonwhite, African American, Latino

The percentage of nonwhite players has risen in Major League Baseball overall, but the demographic shifts have seen African American and Latino percentages head in opposite directions.

WHERE ARE THE NONWHITE MANAGERS?

Beyond the player numbers, MLB has a noticeable lack of racial and ethnic diversity among team managers. Of the 30 teams at the start of the 2018 season, only four had managers of color (three Latinos and one African American), for just 13 percent of the total. That is down significantly from a high of ten nonwhite managers in 2009.

If one believes that diversity among the manager ranks should mirror that of the league's players, approximately 13 teams should have nonwhite managers. MLB has never hit that number, and in fact it is moving in the opposite direction.

There may be several reasons for the lack of nonwhite managers. Some cite a shift in the types of general managers (GMs) teams are hiring to run their operations. Many teams have followed the trend of hiring younger GMs who tend to focus more on statistics and technology than scouting and relationships. Those GMs in turn are more likely to hire younger, analytics-minded managers instead of the older, more experienced managers found in baseball's minor leagues. Minor league managers have traditionally been a more diverse group, while the new-style managers are more likely to be white.

Other experts note that teams continue to rely on their own inner circles when identifying manager candidates, rather than looking beyond their standard talent pool—a practice that favors whites over minorities. This is true even with the shift toward younger GMs, who tend to come from a small number of elite universities.

Dusty Baker managed four MLB teams after a 19-year career as a player. He noted that modern-day managers follow a much different path than he and most of his contemporaries did. "I ask guys all the time, 'Man, how'd you get hired?' This guy went to school with this guy, he went to Amherst, he went to Harvard, he went to Stanford," Baker said. "With just Ivy League guys running the game, mostly, I've noticed that most of them hire the farm directors. The people in the organization are former guys they went to school with, their fraternity brothers, and most of us don't really have that connection. Most of us weren't at that school and most of us that played baseball weren't in the fraternity."[7]

SUCCESSFUL MANAGERS OF COLOR

Many minority managers have seen success in MLB. In 1992, Cito Gaston of the Toronto Blue Jays became the first black manager to win the World Series, and he won his second title the following year. And in 2005, Venezuelan Ozzie Guillén guided the Chicago White Sox to their first World Series victory since 1917.

Some also believe that teams have not done a good job of proactively looking for African American and Latino manager candidates the way the NFL has done

Dusty Baker managed the Washington Nationals in 2016 and 2017.

since the Rooney Rule was implemented. "I think one of the issues that we've had in the game in the past as an industry collectively, we have not done a very good job of recruitment," said Kevan Graves, assistant general manager for the Pittsburgh Pirates. "I think it's in large part because we haven't had to. We have an incredibly large pool of talented, hungry, motivated folks who approach clubs, the Pirates included, unprompted. As you divide your efforts and your energy and your time, I don't think a lot of resources have been committed [to finding minority candidates]."[8]

ADDRESSING THE ISSUE

Recognizing the league's diversity issues, MLB has over time introduced a series of programs designed to increase the number of nonwhite players in the league. They include the Reviving Baseball in Inner Cities (RBI) program, the Play Ball initiative, and MLB Youth Academies. To help attract more nonwhite managers, the league in 1999 implemented what came to be known as the Selig Rule, which is similar to the NFL's Rooney Rule. The Selig Rule, named after former MLB commissioner Bud Selig, requires teams to interview at least one minority candidate for all high-ranking positions, including team manager; it does not mandate that teams hire a minority candidate.

Unlike in the NFL, however, this rule has not had a lasting impact on baseball's minority hiring, as noted by the decline in the number of minority managers in the league. "I think baseball needs to be concerned. Just bringing in a diverse pool of candidates has not produced the numbers they want," said Richard Lapchick, director of the Institute for Diversity and Ethics in Sport. "The number is low enough and has been low enough for the past couple years

TOP TALENT SHINES IN NEGRO LEAGUES

Baseball has long been known as "America's game," and that extended to black Americans as well, even if they were initially barred from playing in the major leagues. To accommodate the growing interest from black fans, Andrew "Rube" Foster in 1920 formed the Negro National League. All-black leagues formed in other parts of the country, and in many years the top teams in each league faced one another in the Negro World Series. The Negro Leagues attracted the best minority players in the country, and the talent level rivaled that of the all-white major leagues.

When MLB felt pressure to integrate after World War II (1939–1945), it raided the Negro Leagues for talent. The first black player to make the leap was Jackie Robinson of the Negro American League's Kansas City Monarchs. He signed with the Brooklyn Dodgers in 1946 and debuted the next year. Other black players, many of whom ended up in the National Baseball Hall of Fame, followed, bringing their black fans with them—and finally making Major League Baseball a game for all Americans.

that there has got to be a way to come up with a bigger hiring pool."[9]

To address this continuing issue, in 2016 MLB created a new Diversity Pipeline Program designed to enlarge the pool of qualified minority candidates at all levels, including both managers and front office staff. This program is run by former Pittsburgh Pirates director of player personnel Tyrone Brooks. He tries to identify and prepare potential managers and connect them with teams in the league. As Brooks explains, the program can serve as a bridge between a player's days on the field and potential opportunities at different levels of an organization.

I've been able to have a lot of different discussions with individuals, those that either, their playing career is coming to an end, or those that are in schools and may not know the whole pathway, how to go about this process to work in our game. So then I'm able to . . . pass their names and information over to [teams] so they can make sure they're in their pool as they're trying to decide who they're going to hire.[10]

Progress is also being made in other coaching positions. Across the league, about 44 percent of all other coaches, such as hitting and pitching coaches, are people of color.[11] That's more than double what it was in 1993, when only 20 percent of major league coaches were nonwhite.

DISCUSSION STARTERS

- Why do you think MLB is less diverse than the NBA and NFL?
- Do MLB owners need to consider their fans' concerns when choosing a team manager?
- Why do you think MLB's Selig Rule hasn't been as effective as the NFL's Rooney Rule in bringing more coaches of color into the league?

CHAPTER SIX

MINORITY OWNERSHIP

Pakistani American businessman Shahid Khan purchased the Jacksonville Jaguars in 2011.

P ro sports teams are limited commodities—there are only 92 men's major league teams in baseball, basketball, and football combined. That makes any individual team worth a lot of money when it comes up for sale.

In 2014, for example, former Microsoft chief executive officer (CEO) Steve Ballmer paid $2 billion for the NBA's Los Angeles Clippers. In 2017, legendary Yankees shortstop Derek Jeter and a group of investors paid $1.2 billion for MLB's Florida Marlins. And in 2018, hedge fund manager David Tepper acquired the NFL's Carolina Panthers for a reported $2.2 billion.

The number of people who can afford to pay that kind of money are few and far between, and they're mainly very wealthy white men. As *Washington Post* sports columnist Jerry Brewer observed of the NFL's well-to-do owners, "Ownership diversity is a complicated pursuit because only the wealthiest of the wealthy can afford NFL franchises, and not many minorities have that kind of money."[1]

NONWHITE OWNERS IN PRO SPORTS TODAY

Because of the amount of money it takes to buy a professional sports team, most of these teams are owned by very wealthy families and individuals. There simply aren't that many nonwhite owners in the major leagues today.

The NBA, for example, has only three nonwhite American majority owners among its 30 teams. Just one of these owners is African American—former superstar player Michael Jordan, owner of the Charlotte Hornets. In 2010, he purchased a stake in the team equal to approximately 10 percent. Vivek Ranadivé, an Indian American tech entrepreneur, heads the management group that owns the Sacramento Kings. And Marc Lasry, a Moroccan-born hedge fund manager, is a co-owner of the Milwaukee Bucks.

The NFL has two nonwhite owners. Shahid Khan, owner of the Jacksonville Jaguars, is a Pakistani American who made his fortune running Flex-N-Gate, an auto parts company; he also owns the English soccer club Fulham. Kim Pegula and her husband Terry are co-owners of the Buffalo Bills, which makes her both the only Asian American and the only female majority owner in American major league sports.

WHO HAS THE MONEY?

Historically, the concentration of extreme wealth in America has been represented primarily by white men who either were successful in business or inherited the money from their families. In contrast, there are far fewer people of color (and women) who achieve the highest levels of wealth in this country; *Forbes* magazine listed just three African Americans (Michael Jordan, Oprah Winfrey, and hedge fund mogul Robert Smith) on its 2018 list of billionaires.

MLB has just a single nonwhite majority owner. Mexican American Arturo Moreno, who made his billions in the advertising industry, owns the Los Angeles Angels.

That's just six owners who are not of European ancestry—only one of whom is African American—among America's 92 professional baseball, basketball, and football teams. That means that 93.5 percent of all major professional sports team owners are white.[2]

MINORITY OWNERS OF MINORITY SHARES

A majority owner is someone who controls more than 50 percent of the team. There is somewhat more diversity when one considers minorities who are *minority owners*—those who own less than a 50 percent share of a team.

Obviously, more individuals have the financial resources to acquire a smaller percentage of a pro sports team. If a team is worth $1 billion, for example, a 2 percent share could be had for just $20 million. That is not an insubstantial amount, but certainly more affordable than the entire $1 billion—which opens up more investment opportunities for less enormously wealthy people of any color.

For example, the NBA lists 35 people of color as minority team owners. That list includes 23 African Americans, nine Asian Americans, and three Latinos. Notable nonwhite minority owners in the NBA include former players Grant Hill (Atlanta Hawks) and Shaquille O'Neal (Sacramento Kings), actors Will Smith and Jada Pinkett Smith (Philadelphia 76ers), and Sheila Johnson (Washington Wizards), cofounder of the BET cable network. In Major League Baseball, Jeter owns a minority share of the Miami Marlins, and former basketball star Earvin "Magic" Johnson has a minority stake in the Los Angeles Dodgers. And in the NFL, Latino musicians Gloria Estefan and Marc Anthony own minority shares in the Miami Dolphins, as do tennis legends Serena and Venus Williams.

RACISM IN THE OWNERSHIP RANKS

Given the large concentration of pro sports team ownership in the hands of older white men, it is not surprising that some of these owners have been accused of being racist.

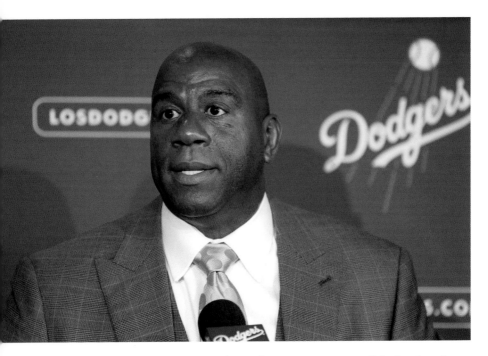

Basketball legend Magic Johnson became part owner of the Los Angeles Dodgers in 2012.

While there is little evidence of widespread racism among team owners, there have been individual instances of owners making racist remarks in the recent past.

One of the most controversial team owners in recent memory was Marge Schott, the owner, president, and CEO of the Cincinnati Reds from 1984 to 1999. Among her numerous offenses, she displayed Nazi memorabilia in her office, referred to one of her black players as her "million-dollar n****r," and called one of the team's marketing directors a "beady-eyed Jew."[3] Schott received hefty fines for her most offensive remarks and was forced by the league in 1999 to sell her shares in the team.

In the NBA, Donald Sterling, then owner of the NBA's Los Angeles Clippers, became notorious for his racist comments. In 2014, audio recordings surfaced in which Sterling criticized his former girlfriend for publicly "associating with black people."[4] The recordings were so offensive that the NBA quickly responded, forcing Sterling to sell the team and banning him from the league for life.

In the NFL, several team owners have been accused of racism based on their response to the player protests started by former San Francisco 49ers quarterback Colin Kaepernick. In a 2016 preseason game, Kaepernick controversially dropped to one knee during the playing of the national anthem, in sympathy with the Black Lives Matter protests against institutional police brutality toward African Americans. Other players followed suit in later games, which angered President Donald Trump, who used the protests to gain political points with his conservative base.

The team owners responded to Trump's challenge by allegedly blacklisting or unofficially banning Kaepernick from the league, as well as implementing a new policy that requires players to either stand or wait in the locker room during the anthem. This policy was viewed by many as a racist response to the protests by primarily black players.

In addition, some team owners were criticized for their individual responses to the issue. Houston Texans owner Robert McNair, for example, said, "We can't have the inmates running the prison," which rather unsubtly compared black football players to convicted criminals.[5]

HOW TO MAKE TEAM OWNERSHIP MORE DIVERSE

However, in the world of professional sports, team ownership does not frequently turn over. Once someone becomes the owner of a pro sports team, he or she is likely to retain ownership for decades. This is especially true in the case of family ownership; a team often is passed down from one family member to another. For example, 22 of the 32 teams in the NFL have been owned by the same person or family for at least 20 years.

When a team does come up for sale, the price is astronomical, which works against efforts to increase diversity in the ownership ranks. If only rich white men can afford to buy professional sports teams, how can the leagues encourage more qualified nonwhite owners?

Ultimately, for professional sports to have more nonwhite owners, African Americans and other minorities have to be given the opportunities to succeed financially that have historically been reserved for white males in our society. As sportswriter and podcaster Riley Nicklaus Evans observed, "It's fairly evident when you look at the history of the United States that for the longest time, people other than white people have been frozen out of the areas of industry that would allow you to accrue the level of wealth required to purchase a professional sports franchise. . . . Once we see more diversity on things like the *Forbes*' [magazine] billionaire lists, we'll start to see more diversity in ownership."[6] Until this societal economic inequality is addressed, ownership of professional sports teams is likely to remain primarily a white men's club.

DISCUSSION STARTERS

- Why do major league sports teams cost so much to buy?
- What racist behavior, if any, have you seen exhibited by owners of MLB, NBA, and NFL teams?
- What can the major sports leagues themselves do to encourage more owners of color?

CHAPTER SEVEN

DIVERSITY IN THE FRONT OFFICE

During the late 1970s and 1980s, Ozzie Newsome was a tight end for the NFL's Cleveland Browns. After his playing career ended, he moved into various front office positions for the Browns, staying with the team when it moved to Baltimore and became the Ravens. In November 2002, Newsome was named GM of the Ravens, making him the first black GM in NFL history.

In pro football, a GM typically oversees all the operations for the organization, hiring and firing players and coaches. In Newsome's case, the GM position came with the added responsibility of being a rare higher-level African American in a league with primarily white senior management. His race makes an impact on the people he deals with on a daily basis and on the players he tries to sign. Newsome once commented, "When people see people of their color in positions like this, there's a warmness."[1]

Newsome has been one of the most successful GMs in NFL history. The teams he helped build won two Super Bowls, and a 2018 USA Today poll of NFL agents named Newsome the most respected decision maker in the league. "You can sit down and have a frank discussion with him," said one agent. "He won't pull punches, but he's fair."[2]

Newsome, right, and Ravens head coach John Harbaugh confer at a team practice in 2017.

Unfortunately, Newsome is a rarity. NFL, NBA, and MLB teams employ few people of color at senior levels—although there is more diversity lower down in the organizations.

DETAILING THE ORGANIZATION

The typical professional sports team is a large organization. It's not just coaches and players; a sports team includes marketing, sales, human resources, and other staff. There's top-level management, such as the president and CEO, as well as recruiters, trainers, dieticians, lawyers, assistants, and interns.

Take, as an example, the corporate staff (sometimes called the front office) of Newsome's Baltimore Ravens. This staff is divided into 20 departments that employ more than 160 people.[3] Other sports teams have a similar structure and staff. That's a good-sized staff for any type of company.

Most sports teams do a decent job of hiring a diverse front office staff—in most cases, even more diverse than the ownership and coaching ranks. However, there remains room for progress—especially at higher levels.

DIVERSITY IN SENIOR MANAGEMENT

The top-level positions in a team's organization are typically referred to as senior management. These include the presidents, vice presidents, GMs, and directors throughout the organization, including but not exclusively the ownership and executive departments. These people, from the top down, define the shape of the organization; a lack of diversity here can contribute to fewer minority hires throughout the organization.

The very top levels of senior management are typically not very diverse. At the start of the 2017–18 season, the NBA had just five CEO/president-level positions held by African Americans.[4] It's worse in the NFL, which had zero people of color at the president or CEO level.[5] And at the start of the 2018 MLB season, no senior-level people of color served in team front offices.[6]

PROGRESSIVE THINKING IN THE NBA

The NBA is universally recognized as the leader among all men's professional sports leagues in terms of diversity. This emphasis on diversity started under former commissioner David Stern, who believed that the racial makeup of the league's management should reflect that of its players. From the beginning of his tenure, Stern stepped up the hiring of minorities and women in the league office, with the ultimate goal that "no one will notice not only when we hire a person of color but also when we fire a person of color." [10] He advocated that the NBA and its players could and should bring about positive social change.

This focus on diversity at all levels has helped expand the league's audience. The NBA is the only major professional sports league in which the percentage of black fans (45 percent) is larger than the percentage of white fans (40 percent). [11] In this instance, diversity on the court and in the front office is reflected by diversity in the stands.

The GM position is also an important senior management job, as the GM handles most of the player-related hiring and firing and can significantly impact the diversity of the player ranks. As with CEO-level positions, however, the GM position is mainly held by white men. In the 2017–18 NBA season, just five people of color (20 percent of all positions) served in the GM role. [7] That number is six (10 percent) in the NFL. [8] Meanwhile, only four (6.7 percent) people of color were GMs in MLB. [9]

Most of the other senior management positions include people with the phrase "vice president" (VP) in their titles. But diversity at the VP level isn't much better than with other senior management positions, with the NBA having

Chicago White Sox vice president Kenny Williams, left, *chats with former manager Ozzie Guillén in 2015.*

the best record with 25.4 percent of its VP slots held by people of color.[12] The NFL was the worst at 10.8 percent.[13]

The unfortunate lack of diversity at the senior management levels of most major league sports teams helps to explain the corresponding lack of diversity further down in the organization and in the coaching ranks. Improving diversity at the top would likely lead to an increase in diversity throughout the entire organization.

DIVERSITY AMONG OTHER TEAM EMPLOYEES

Minority representation is better at lower levels of most organizations for a number of reasons. First, some of these positions are being hired by people of color, who are generally more open to minority hires. Second, many of these jobs are competing with similar jobs outside of the sports world, so the candidates are more reflective of the community's demographics.

Diversity in senior administration positions is significantly better than at a team's senior management levels. Administration positions are typically sports-related jobs but with general skills, such as director, assistant general manager, chief legal counsel, public relations director, and the like. For example, 31.2 percent of senior administration jobs in the NBA are held by people of color.[14] In the NFL, people of color hold 18.2 percent of those positions.[15]

Go down one more level and diversity is even more evident. The professional administration level includes positions with professional skills that transfer directly to similar jobs in the non-sports sector, including assistant director, controller, administrator, and similar jobs. In the NBA, 39.5 percent of these positions are filled by people of color. [16]

IMPROVING DIVERSITY IN THE FRONT OFFICE

While most professional sports teams have increased diversity at lower levels of the organization, work still needs to be done in increasing the number of nonwhite senior staff. The disappointing number of people of color serving in president, vice president, and CEO-level positions clearly reflects on the lack of diversity in the people who hire them—the team owners.

The NFL tried to address this situation with the Rooney Rule. Originally devised to improve diversity at the coaching level, the rule has been revised to also apply to senior operations positions; the rule requires teams to interview at least one minority candidate for any open senior position. MLB took a similar approach with its Selig Rule, which from the start addressed general manager, assistant general manager, field manager, director of player development, and director of scouting positions.

DIVERSITY IN COLLEGE SPORTS

The lack of diversity among front office staff in professional sports mirrors a similar lack of diversity in college sports. As of the fall of 2016, only 12.1 percent of the campus leadership positions in athletics were held by people of color. In contrast, 88.3 percent of college presidents were white, as were 89.4 percent of faculty athletics representatives. Of the ten conference commissioners in the Football Bowl Subdivision (FBS), all were white; there has never been a person of color in this position.[17]

This poor record of diversity led the NCAA to adopt *The Pledge and Commitment to Promoting Diversity and Gender in Intercollegiate Athletics*. Supporting schools pledge to "commit to establishing initiatives for achieving ethnic and racial diversity, gender equity and inclusion, with a focus and emphasis on hiring practices in intercollegiate athletics."[18]

As of July 2018, 862 schools and 102 conferences have signed this nonbinding pledge. Whether the NCAA's efforts in this area will be enough to improve diversity in college sports remains to be seen.

The NBA does not have a similar hiring rule, although some believe it might be a good idea to do so. Michele Roberts, executive director of the National Basketball Players Association, said, "I don't know if we necessarily need to replicate football with the mandatory interviews of GMs and coaches of color. It couldn't hurt. But we have to do something."[19]

But simply enacting this kind of rule does not guarantee that teams actually hire minority candidates for these positions, as witnessed by the relative lack of diversity among NFL senior management. Roberts and others believe that the lack of nonwhite team owners affects the number of people of color hired for senior management positions. If team ownership were more diverse, the owners would likely hire more nonwhite front office management.

DISCUSSION STARTERS

- If you worked in the front office for a major league sports team, how would you try to convince management to increase organizational diversity?
- How would you feel if you thought you were qualified for a job but didn't get a chance to interview for it? Would you wonder if your race had anything to do with it?
- Why do you think the NBA has a better record of diversity in the front office than the NFL or MLB?

INTEGRATING LEAGUE MANAGEMENT AND PLAYERS' UNIONS

I n 2014, Mark Tatum was named the NBA's deputy commissioner and chief operating officer. That's the number two position in the league office, the group of people who run the league. Tatum reports directly to the commissioner. This makes him the highest-ranking racial minority in any American professional sports league.

Tatum has worked for the NBA since 1999, holding a variety of senior-level positions. In his current role, he is responsible for all of the NBA's business operations, including leading the league's international efforts.

As the son of two immigrants—a Jamaican father and Vietnamese mother—Tatum recognizes the importance of diversity in an organization.

"What I found is that the more diverse a community is, the stronger it is, the more perspectives you get, the better decisions that you make, and we see that in the business world as well," Tatum says.[1]

DIVERSITY AT LEAGUE OFFICES

In general, diversity at league offices is greater than with the individual teams. Tatum is reflective of that and has personally helped diversify the NBA league office at all levels, making it the most diverse of all major league

Troy Vincent is the NFL's executive vice president of football operations.

offices. At the end of the 2017–18 season, 36.4 percent of professional staff positions at the NBA league office were held by people of color—16.8 percent were held by African Americans, 5.9 percent by Latinos, and 10 percent by Asian Americans. This is a much higher minority representation than at the NBA team level.[2]

At the NFL league office, 28.4 percent of those management positions were held by people of color at the start of the 2017 season. This includes African Americans (8.9 percent), Latinos (7.5 percent), and Asian Americans

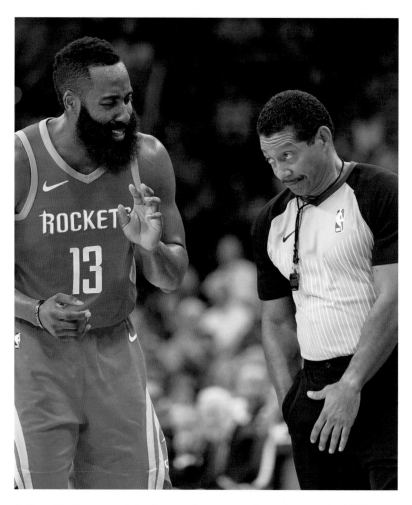

Referee Bill Kennedy, right, is one of many people of color on the NBA's officiating staff.

(8.6 percent).[3] While not quite as diverse as the NBA league office, it is still significantly more diverse than the staff at individual NFL teams.

The MLB league office is almost as diverse as the NBA league office, and 33.8 percent of the professional staff are people of color. That includes 10.1 percent

African Americans, 14.9 percent Latinos, and 5.7 percent Asian Americans.[4]

As the three league offices continue to hire racially and ethnically diverse staff at all levels, that presents a positive image and helps to inspire the individual teams in each league. Working with and seeing the success of minority staff at the league office shows the teams' senior management the value of diversity and hopefully encourages them to further diversify their own staffs. In addition, diverse league staffs are likely to pursue proactive diversity efforts across the leagues.

DIVERSITY IN OFFICIATING STAFF

One often-overlooked function of league operations is the hiring and management of the officiating staff—the referees and umpires who work the thousands of games each year. Some of the leagues have a diverse officiating staff; others, not quite so much.

In the NBA, for example, 56.2 percent of the league's referees in the 2017–18 season were people of color. In the NFL, 30.6 percent of field officials were people of color. But in MLB, only 11 percent of the umpires were people of color—an obvious diversity issue in that league, and one that reflects the relative lack of diversity in other baseball management positions.[5]

MLB'S FIRST BLACK UMPIRE

The first black umpire in Major League Baseball was Emmett Ashford, who officiated the opening day game between the Washington Senators and Cleveland Indians on April 11, 1966. He started officiating in 1951 in the Southwestern International League and worked his way up through multiple other minor leagues over the next 15 years.

After all the initial publicity, Ashford soon became a favorite with the fans. He was known for his energetic style and karate-like chop when calling strikes.

Ironically, when he tried to enter the umpire's room at DC Stadium for his first game, Ashford was stopped by an FBI agent guarding the door. "I told him I was an umpire," Ashford said. "He said there aren't any Negro umpires in the majors. So I told him, 'There won't be if you don't let me go.'"[6] The agent relented, and Ashford made history.

Any attempt to improve diversity among officials is likely to take some time, if only because the path to major league officiating is a long one. In MLB, for example, it can take ten years or more for an umpire to progress through the minor leagues to take a spot in the majors—and then only when a position opens up.

One possible issue with having white officials making calls against nonwhite players is whether there is any innate prejudice that influences the outcome of those calls. In MLB, for example, 81 out of 91 umpires—89 percent—are white, making calls against the 42.5 percent of players who are nonwhite. If the white umpires unfairly judged against the nonwhite players, it could affect the outcome of the games.

A 2011 study called *Strike Three: Discrimination, Incentives, and Evaluation,* by professors from three different universities, examined this issue. The study found some evidence of discrimination by umpires against pitchers of a different race. According to this study, an umpire, with all other factors being equal, calls a pitch a strike about 1 percent more often if he and the pitcher are of the same race.[7] Two later studies, however, found any such discrimination to be minimal and possibly explained by other factors.[8]

Similar research into officiating in the NBA, reported in *Racial Discrimination among NBA Referees* by Joseph Price and Justin Wolfers, came out in 2007. It found that white officials call fouls against black players slightly more frequently than they do against white players. One of the study's authors called this difference "small, subtle, and significant."[9] Seven years later, however, the same researchers revisited the

INSIDE THE PLAYERS' UNIONS

While the league offices exist to service the teams and their owners as well as the players in the league, players' unions solely represent the needs of the players. The heads of these labor unions negotiate contracts between the league and the players, represent players when they have issues with their teams or the league, and manage the players' health and retirement plans. They also work to promote a positive image for the players and assist various community organizations and charities.

DeMaurice Smith was elected executive director of the NFL's players' union in 2009.

updated numbers and found the difference largely gone. Even though the original bias was small, once it was pointed out to the league, the referees adjusted and the bias was eliminated.

What does all this mean? White officials may have a bias toward white players, although that bias is likely to be small. Still, efforts to diversify the race and ethnicity of game officials is worth pursuing.

DIVERSITY IN THE PLAYERS' UNIONS

As the player rosters in all major league sports teams are heavily nonwhite, it follows that the management of the players' unions are equally diverse. As of 2018, the heads of all three major players' unions are African American. Michele Roberts is the executive director of the National Basketball Players Association, DeMaurice Smith is the executive director of the NFL Players Association, and Tony Clark is the executive director of the MLB Players Association. They each represent the needs of a diverse group of current and former players.

Roberts, especially, is an outspoken advocate for the 400 or so players she represents—the vast majority of whom are black. She also has to deal with the challenges of being not just a person of color but also the first female director of any professional players' union.

DISCUSSION STARTERS

- If you were the NBA commissioner, would you work harder to keep the team owners or the players happy? And why?
- How might a person's race or national background affect his or her ability to referee a sports game?
- Why do you think the WNBA has such a good record for diversity?

DIVERSITY IN
THE WNBA

Professional basketball is unique in that it has parallel men's and women's leagues. And the Women's National Basketball Association (WNBA) is even more diverse than the men's league. Many consider the WNBA to be the leader in both racial and gender diversity among all major sports leagues.

WNBA president Lisa Borders

During the 2018 season, the 12-team WNBA had three black head coaches for 25 percent of the league total. Six head coaches were women, including two black women.

Not surprisingly, 41.2 percent of the league's professional positions were held by women, while 26.7 percent of all positions were held by minorities. Six women were general managers, and five held CEO/president positions. Three general managers were people of color and three held CEO/president positions.[10] Lisa Borders, an African American woman, is the president of the league.

Katrina Adams, chair, CEO, and president of the United States Tennis Association, commented, "The WNBA is to be commended for its continuing commitment to diversity and inclusion through all levels of the association. They set a very high bar, and are clearly the industry standard."[11]

The Indiana Fever hired head coach Pokey Chatman in 2016.

CHAPTER NINE

FIGHTING THE STEREOTYPES

Increasing diversity in professional sports has been and continues to be a challenge at all levels. Some leagues have more coaches and managers of color than do others, but all can improve the number of minorities in top-level roles in their organizations.

The NBA, the NFL, and MLB all recognize this, and all have programs in place to attract more people of color to key positions. There is much more that can be done, however.

WORKING FROM THE TOP DOWN

Within any organization, significant cultural change often comes from the top down, dictated by the company's CEO, president, or owner. If a league wants to improve diversity in its ranks, it should look first at its team owners.

Most experts believe that having more owners of color should lead to more diversity in both front office management and coaching staff. Just as the teams' white owners tend to hire white CEOs and head coaches, exacerbating the current diversity problem, an owner of color might hire more nonwhite managers and coaches. In this way of thinking, diversity starts at the top.

Rapper, fashion mogul, and businessman Sean Combs came up short in his attempt to purchase the NFL's Carolina Panthers in 2017.

Unfortunately, there is currently and historically a lack of people of color among the team owners. Pro sports teams today are so expensive that ownership favors the wealthiest of the wealthy, and the wealthiest of the wealthy in our country are predominantly white. As sports attorney Richard Roth notes, "Historically the wealth in this country belongs to white males. It's the same reason most Fortune 500 companies, most law firms, etc. are owned by white males."[1]

Consider the situation in 2017 when the NFL's Carolina Panthers were put on the sales block. One of the initial candidates for acquiring the team was hip-hop musician Sean Combs (a.k.a. Diddy), who would have become the first black owner of an NFL team, but he simply didn't have enough money to compete in the bidding. While Combs's net worth was a respectable $820 million, bidding for the team rose to $2.2 billion, putting it well out of his reach. The team was eventually purchased by David Tepper, a white hedge fund manager with a personal net worth of $11 billion. Not even a wildly successful music mogul makes enough money to afford an NFL team.

Unfortunately, the league offices can't control the sky-high pricing when teams go up for sale—but they can do more to help people of color invest in team ownership. Given the astronomical cost of buying a sports team, it's likely that more future owners will actually be ownership *groups* composed of multiple minority owners (and perhaps a single lead majority owner). For those people of color who want to own a pro sports team but don't have the necessary net worth, being part of an ownership group is a good solution—and one that can more quickly improve the diversity of the ownership ranks.

For all practical purposes, however, a top-down solution to the ownership problem could take years or even decades to implement. This is why the leagues need to continue to address diversity at the next levels down, with coaches and front office management.

WORKING FROM THE BOTTOM UP

More immediate success can be had by working from the bottom up, by increasing the pool of qualified candidates for mid- and high-level team positions. One example of working from the bottom up is the NBA's Basketball Operations Associate Program, which grooms qualified candidates for future management roles. The goal of this yearlong program is to help former players develop the business skills they need for these front office positions. NBA deputy commissioner Mark Tatum notes that they can "work with the [National Basketball Players Association] and players or recently retired players interested in getting into the business of basketball or the operations side and put them

CULTURE OF INCLUSION

To improve diversity in the NBA, some suggest that the league should adopt its own version of the Rooney Rule. Others, such as Otis Stuart, the NBA's senior vice president and chief diversity and inclusion officer, suggest that a more subtle cultural change is required. "We know, of course, of the Rooney Rule," Stuart says. "We celebrate the fact that the NFL has implemented that before. But with us, we have to do something that will work for our unique situation. Focus on culture that we believe will create a sustainable outcome, one that is not based on just a process or that kind of oversight. . . . It's about a culture of inclusion that will ultimately start a sustainable process that is going to really address that issue."[2]

in this program to give them exposure to what it takes to be a general manager in this league."[3]

Out of the office and onto the court, another option is to provide additional training for former players who want to join the coaching ranks. The NBA has hired a number of African American former players as head coaches in the past, and the results have not been uniformly positive. Part of the reason is that these former players moved into head coaching positions without any training or previous experience. Some have thrived on their natural abilities, but others have not. Providing additional training as well as access to assistant coaching positions could improve the prospects for any player turned coach.

The NFL has several programs designed to improve diversity. The NFL Diversity Council works with the league's commissioner and executive team to create policies and programs that build diversity awareness across the league. The NFL Career Advisory Panel helps to identify top candidates for open coaching positions, with a special emphasis on minority candidates. The Bill Walsh Diversity Fellowship Program utilizes team training camps, off-season workout programs, and mini camps to provide minority coaches with opportunities to observe, participate, and hopefully gain full-time coaching positions. In addition, the league has a recruiting website designed to attract talented

MINORITIES IN THE MINOR LEAGUES

In baseball, there is significantly more diversity in the minor leagues than in the majors. One report claims that about 30 percent of minor league managers are people of color; that is more than double the percentage of nonwhite managers in the major leagues.[4] This is possibly due to minor league teams being more open to hiring ex-players, who are more likely to be black or Hispanic. There is also the issue of lower salaries (and lower expectations) in the minors, which gives minority managers more breathing room than in the majors.

The high number of Latino managers is particularly helpful when it comes to working with rookie players from outside the United States. Jolbert Cabrera, manager of the South Atlantic League's Augusta GreenJackets, a Class A team, notes, "It's useful to have bilingual managers on the lower level to help players when they come from Spanish-speaking countries."[5]

This level of diversity in baseball's minor leagues should eventually help improve diversity in the National and American Leagues. The 30 major league teams often draw from their minor league teams to fill not only player but also coaching positions. The minors are a good training ground for talented individuals, and the more people of color who gain experience there, the more people of color the majors are likely to hire.

people of color; it acts as a database of potential candidates interested in career opportunities across the league.

MLB, which faces the most severe diversity challenges, offers multiple programs to attract more minority candidates at all levels. For example, the Diversity Pipeline Program aims to identify and grow the pool of minority and female candidates for a variety of on- and off-field positions. Under this program, each team is required to provide a plan for increasing the diversity of its staff. And the league offers

Former MLB commissioner Bud Selig was a major proponent of the league's RBI program.

several initiatives designed to attract more minority youths to the sport, including the Play Ball and Reviving Baseball in Inner Cities (RBI) programs.

The key with these bottom-up initiatives is to attract more people of color to entry-level and above positions, and to train and prepare these candidates adequately for their future roles. When positions open up, people in this pool will be better equipped to handle the challenges and thus successfully increase diversity throughout the leagues.

STRIVING FOR DIVERSITY

However professional sports leagues and teams work to improve diversity in their ranks, the goal is an admirable and important one. It is essential that professional sports move from a white-dominated hierarchy to one that better reflects the multiracial makeup of their players, their fans, and their communities. The days of white men ruling sports are fading into the past as America becomes less white and more diverse. Fans want to see teams that represent all races, ethnicities, and cultures, and that means hiring more diverse players and staff at all levels. Professional sports teams run by a diverse staff will go a long way toward helping those teams inspire, connect with, and gain support from their fans and local communities.

DISCUSSION STARTERS

- Can teams truly improve diversity under mostly white team ownership and management?
- How would you change the Rooney Rule to make it more effective?
- What types of programs could the leagues adopt to encourage team offices to hire more people of color?

ESSENTIAL FACTS

SIGNIFICANT EVENTS

○ In 1966, Bill Russell is appointed head coach of the NBA's Boston Celtics, becoming the first black coach in the NBA and in all of modern-day professional sports.

○ Frank Robinson is named manager of the Cleveland Indians in October 1974, becoming the first black manager of modern-day professional baseball.

○ In 1989, Art Shell takes over as head coach of the Oakland Raiders, becoming the first black head coach in the modern era of the NFL.

○ The NFL enacts the Rooney Rule in 2003 to encourage the hiring of more head coaches of color.

○ In 2010, Michael Jordan purchases a nearly 10 percent stake in the NBA's Charlotte Hornets, becoming the first African American owner of an American major league sports team.

KEY PLAYERS

○ Dan Rooney is the former owner of the Pittsburgh Steelers and chairman of the NFL's diversity committee. He headed a group that lobbied for more minority representation in the league's coaching ranks. (The resulting Rooney Rule was named after him.)

○ Tony Dungy is the former head coach of the Tampa Bay Buccaneers and the Indianapolis Colts and the first black head coach to win the Super Bowl. Dungy was responsible for bringing a large amount of minority talent into the NFL.

○ Tyrone Brooks, senior director of MLB's Front Office and Field Staff Diversity Program, is responsible for stimulating greater diversity in baseball's executive levels.

- Michele Roberts, executive director of the National Basketball Players Association, is the chief advocate for the approximately 400 players in the NBA.

- Mark Tatum is the deputy commissioner and chief operating officer for the NBA. He is second only to the commissioner in the league office and is the highest ranking African American in any American professional sports league.

IMPACT ON SOCIETY

Professional sports leagues and teams need to better reflect the racial and ethnic diversity of their players, fans, and communities. Increasing diversity in the coaching and management ranks helps a team to better connect with its fans (and increase its fan base) and to improve support from its local community. In addition, having coaching and management mirror the diversity of a team's player roster helps to attract more talented players and makes it easier to lead them more effectively.

QUOTE

"What I found is that the more diverse a community is, the stronger it is, the more perspectives you get, the better decisions that you make."

—Mark Tatum, NBA deputy commissioner and chief operating officer

GLOSSARY

CEO
Short for chief executive officer, the person with the main decision-making authority in an organization.

coordinator
In football, the person who coordinates and manages all offensive or defensive coaches; second-in-command to the team's head coach.

diversity
The inclusion of different types of people (of different races, genders, disability statuses, and cultures) in an organization.

front office
The off-field management operations of a sports team.

general manager
For most sports teams, the person responsible for all hiring and firing decisions for players and coaches.

head coach
In the NBA and NFL, the highest-ranking member of the coaching staff, the leader of the team. (In baseball, the head coach is called the manager.)

league office
The central office of a professional sports league that serves both the league's teams and its players.

manager

In baseball, the head coach.

minority owner

A team owner whose share of a team is less than 50 percent.

Negro Leagues

The pre-1960s segregated baseball leagues that featured exclusively black players and managers.

players' union

The labor union that represents a league's players.

prejudice

A preconceived judgment or opinion, typically of a particular race, ethnicity, or gender.

racism

Poor treatment of or violence against people because of their race.

Rooney Rule

The rule in the NFL that requires teams to interview at least one minority candidate for any open coaching or senior front office position.

senior management

The top-level positions in a team's front office organization.

ADDITIONAL RESOURCES

SELECTED BIBLIOGRAPHY

Beck, Howard. "Where Are All the Black NBA Coaches? Examining a Sudden, Silent Disappearance." *Bleacher Report*, 6 Nov. 2015. bleacherreport.com. Accessed 10 July 2018.

Chang, Alvin. "This Is Why Baseball Is So White." *Vox*, 24 Oct. 2017. vox.com. Accessed 10 July 2018.

Levy, Dan. "Coaching Diversity Is an Issue in All American Sports, Not Just the NFL." *Bleacher Report*, 7 Feb. 2013. bleacherreport.com. Accessed 10 July 2018.

Moore, Louis. "The Black NFL Coach Can Be a Clean-Up Man, but He Won't Be Recycled." *The Shadow League*, 7 Jan. 2018. theshadowleague.com. Accessed 10 July 2018.

Shaikin, Bill. "Major League Baseball Is 'Failing' in Its Attempt to Increase Front-Office Diversity and the Issue Could Get Worse." *Los Angeles Times*, 30 June 2017. latimes.com. Accessed 10 July 2018.

Spears, Marc J. "The Distressing Lack of Black Leadership in the NBA." *The Undefeated*, 1 June 2016. theundefeated.com. Accessed 10 July 2018.

FURTHER READINGS

Harris, Duchess, and Kate Conley. *Gender and Race in Sports*. Abdo, 2019.

Skipper, John C. *Frank Robinson: A Baseball Biography*. McFarland, 2015.

ONLINE RESOURCES

To learn more about race and sports management, visit abdobooklinks.com. These links are routinely monitored and updated to provide the most current information available.

MORE INFORMATION

For more information on this subject, contact or visit the following organizations:

NATIONAL COALITION AGAINST RACISM IN SPORTS AND MEDIA (NCARSM)
1113 East Franklin Ave., Suite 103
Minneapolis, MN 55404
612-886-2107
coalitionagainstracism.org

This organization educates about and confronts racism in sports and media. It is known for sponsoring demonstrations outside sports stadiums, as well as promoting an educational effort that addresses the issue of racial stereotyping.

ROSS INITIATIVE IN SPORTS FOR EQUALITY (RISE)
423 W. 55th St., Twelfth Floor
New York, NY 10019
646-582-2350
risetowin.org

This organization, founded by Miami Dolphins owner Stephen M. Ross, is dedicated to improving race relations and driving social progress in the world of sports. RISE provides student athletes, coaches, and administrators with the skills and resources to stand up to racism in sports.

SOURCE NOTES

CHAPTER 1. BREAKING BARRIERS: BILL RUSSELL

1. Bob Bachelder. "That Boston Celtics Death Certificate: Don't Sign It Yet." *Bleacher Report*, 18 Apr. 2009. bleacherreport.com. Accessed 13 Sept. 2018.

2. Matthew Richer. "Busing's Boston Massacre." *Hoover Institution*, 1 Nov. 1998. hoover.org. Accessed 13 Sept. 2018.

3. Doug Merlino. "Bill Russell, Civil Rights Hero and Inventor of Airborne Basketball." *Bleacher Report*, 29 Apr. 2011. bleacherreport.com. Accessed 13 Sept. 2018.

4. John Taylor. *The Rivalry: Bill Russell, Wilt Chamberlain, and the Golden Age of Basketball*. Random, 2005. 264–272.

5. Louis Moore. "The Black NFL Coach Can Be a Clean-Up Man, but He Won't Be Recycled." *Shadow League*, 7 Jan. 2018. theshadowleague.com. Accessed 13 Sept. 2018.

6. "Bill Russell's First Day of Boston Celtics Training Camp as Player-Coach." *YouTube*, uploaded by Wilt Chamberlain Archive, 20 June 2017. youtube.com. Accessed 13 Sept. 2018.

7. Bill Russell and Taylor Branch. *Second Wind: The Memoirs of an Opinionated Man*. Ballantine, 1979. 149.

8. "Bill Russell." *Academy of Achievement*, 15 June 2018. achievement.org. Accessed 13 Sept. 2018.

CHAPTER 2. WHY DIVERSITY MATTERS

1. Grahame L. Jones. "Dodgers Fire Campanis over Racial Remarks." *Los Angeles Times*, 9 Apr. 1987. articles.latimes.com. Accessed 13 Sept. 2018.

2. "The Racial & Gender Report Card." *The Institute for Diversity and Ethics in Sport*, n.d. tidesport.org. Accessed 13 Sept. 2018.

3. Jason Reid. "Rethinking the NFL's Rooney Rule for More Diversity at the Top." *FiveThirtyEight*, 20 May 2016. fivethirtyeight.com. Accessed 13 Sept. 2018.

4. Bill Brink. "MLB Has a Diversity Problem, and It Goes Beyond the Rosters," *Pittsburgh Post-Gazette*, 21 Aug. 2017. post-gazette.com. Accessed 13 Sept. 2018.

5. Mike Sando. "Rooney Rule in Reverse: Minority Coaching Hires Have Stalled." *ESPN*, 19 July 2016. espn.com. Accessed 13 Sept. 2018.

6. "QuickFacts." *United States Census Bureau*, n.d. census.gov. Accessed 13 Sept. 2018.

7. George B. Cunningham. "Diversity Training in Intercollegiate Athletics." *Journal of Sport Management*, vol. 26, no. 5, 2012. 393.

CHAPTER 3. RISING THROUGH THE NBA RANKS

1. Rick Maese. "Over Four Days, the Donald Sterling Story Led to Seismic Changes to Los Angeles Basketball and the NBA." *Washington Post*, 30 Apr. 2014. washingtonpost.com. Accessed 13 Sept. 2018.

2. Howard Beck. "Where Are All the Black NBA Coaches? Examining a Sudden, Silent Disappearance." *Bleacher Report*, 6 Nov. 2015. bleacherreport.com. Accessed 13 Sept. 2018.

3. Beck, "Where Are All the Black NBA Coaches?"

4. Richard Lapchick. "The 2018 Racial and Gender Report Card: National Basketball Association." *Institute for Diversity and Ethics in Sport*, 26 June 2018. tidesport.org. Accessed 13 Sept. 2018.

5. Noah Gulliver. "The Truth about Why Mark Jackson Was Fired." *EveryJoe*, 6 May 2014. everyjoe.com. Accessed 13 Sept. 2018.

6. Beck, "Where Are All the Black NBA Coaches?"

7. Beck, "Where Are All the Black NBA Coaches?"

CHAPTER 4. GRIDIRON GUIDANCE

1. Richard Lapchick. "The 2017 Racial and Gender Report Card: National Football League." *Institute for Diversity and Ethics in Sport*, 18 Oct. 2017. tidesport.org. Accessed 13 Sept. 2018.

2. Jean Desronvil. "NFL African-American Head Coaches Win. Hire Them." *Good Men Project*, 12 Aug. 2016. goodmenproject.com. Accessed 23 Sept. 2018.

3. Louis Moore. "The Black NFL Coach Can Be a Clean-Up Man, but He Won't Be Recycled." *Shadow League*, 7 Jan. 2018. theshadowleague.com. Accessed 13 Sept. 2018.

4. Mike Sando. "The 10 Key Limbs of Tony Dungy's Coaching Tree." *ESPN*, 5 Aug. 2016. espn.com. Accessed 13 Sept. 2018.

5. Jason Reid. "Rethinking the NFL's Rooney Rule for More Diversity at the Top." *FiveThirtyEight*, 20 May 2016. fivethirtyeight.com. Accessed 13 Sept. 2018.

6. Cameron Wolfe. "Climbing a Slippery Mountain: Why NFL's Black Offensive Coaches Struggle to Become a Head Coach, Coordinator." *Denver Post*, 11 Sept. 2017. denverpost.com. Accessed 13 Sept. 2018.

7. Wolfe, "Climbing a Slippery Mountain."

CHAPTER 5. FROM THE DIAMOND TO THE DUGOUT

1. "Jackie Robinson—Last Words." *Biography.com*, n.d., biography.com. Accessed 13 Sept. 2018.

2. Richard Lapchick. "The 2018 Racial and Gender Report Card: Major League Baseball." *Institute for Diversity and Ethics in Sport*, 12 Apr. 2018. tidesport.org. Accessed 13 Sept. 2018.

3. Mark Armour and Daniel R. Levitt. "Baseball Demographics, 1947–2016." *Society for American Baseball Research*, n.d. sabr.org. Accessed 13 Sept. 2018.

4. Richard Lapchick. "MLB Race and Gender Report Card Shows Progress Still Needed." *ESPN*, 18 Apr. 2017. espn.com. Accessed 13 Sept. 2018.

5. Armour and Levitt, "Baseball Demographics."

6. Lapchick. "The 2018 Racial and Gender Report Card: Major League Baseball."

7. Bill Brink. "MLB Has a Diversity Problem, and It Goes beyond the Rosters." *Pittsburgh Post-Gazette*, 21 Aug. 2017. post-gazette.com. Accessed 13 Sept. 2018.

8. Brink, "MLB Has a Diversity Problem."

9. Bill Shaikin. "Major League Baseball Is 'Failing' in Its Attempt to Increase Front-Office Diversity and the Issue Could Get Worse." *Los Angeles Times*, 30 June 2017. latimes.com. Accessed 13 Sept. 2018.

10. Brink, "MLB Has a Diversity Problem."

11. Alvin Chang. "This Is Why Baseball Is So White." *Vox*, 24 Oct. 2017. vox.com. Accessed 13 Sept. 2018.

SOURCE NOTES CONTINUED

CHAPTER 6. MINORITY OWNERSHIP

1. Jerry Brewer. "The NFL Is in Need of Vision. Its Owners Can't See through the White-Out." *Washington Post*, 19 Dec. 2017. washingtonpost.com. Accessed 5 July 2018.

2. Ahiza Garcia. "These Are the Only Two Owners of Color in the NFL." *CNN Money*, 18 May 2018. money.cnn.com. Accessed 13 Sept. 2018.

3. Matt Connolly and AJ Vicens. "4 More Super-Racist Team Owners." *Mother Jones*, 29 Apr. 2014. motherjones.com. Accessed 13 Sept. 2018.

4. Bill Chappell. "NBA Probes 'Disturbing and Offensive' Comments Attributed to Clippers Owner." *NPR*, 26 Apr. 2014. npr.org. Accessed 13 Sept. 2018.

5. Matt Bonesteel. "'We Can't Have the Inmates Running the Prison': Anti-Protest NFL Owners Are Fighting a Losing Battle." *Washington Post*, 27 Oct. 2017. washingtonpost.com. Accessed 13 Sept. 2018.

6. Riley Nicklaus Evans. "The Good, the Bad, and the Extremely-White Men Who Own Sports Teams." *Schtick to Sports*, 20 Feb. 2018. grandstandcentral.com. Accessed 13 Sept. 2018.

CHAPTER 7. DIVERSITY IN THE FRONT OFFICE

1. Domonique Foxworth. "Ozzie Newsome on His Journey from Alabama to NFL History." *Undefeated*, 25 Apr. 2018. theundefeated.com. Accessed 13 Sept. 2018.

2. Jarrett Bell. "What *USA Today* Sports' Poll of NFL Agents Revealed about Bill Belichick, Bruce Allen, and More." *USA Today*, 19 Apr. 2018. usatoday.com. Accessed 13 Sept. 2018.

3. "Front Office Roster," *Baltimore Ravens*, n.d. baltimoreravens.com. Accessed 13 Sept. 2018.

4. Richard Lapchick. "The 2018 Racial and Gender Report Card: National Basketball Association." *Institute for Diversity and Ethics in Sport*, 26 June 2018. tidesport.org. Accessed 13 Sept. 2018.

5. Richard Lapchick. "The 2017 Racial and Gender Report Card: National Football League." *Institute for Diversity and Ethics in Sport*, 18 Oct. 2017. tidesport.org. Accessed 18 June 2018.

6. Richard Lapchick. "The 2018 Racial and Gender Report Card: Major League Baseball." *Institute for Diversity and Ethics in Sport*, 12 Apr. 2018. tidesport.org. Accessed 18 June 2018.

7. Lapchick, "The 2018 Racial and Gender Report Card: National Basketball Association."

8. Lapchick, "The 2017 Racial and Gender Report Card: National Football League."

9. Lapchick, "The 2018 Racial and Gender Report Card: Major League Baseball."

10. Richard Lapchick. "Stern's Legacy Is Diversity, Giving." *ESPN*, 1 Feb. 2014. espn.com. Accessed 13 Sept. 2018.

11. "Year in Sports Media Report: 2013." *Nielsen*, 2014. nielsen.com. Accessed 13 Sept. 2018.

12. Lapchick, "The 2018 Racial and Gender Report Card: National Basketball Association."

13. Lapchick, "The 2017 Racial and Gender Report Card: National Football League."

14. Lapchick, "The 2018 Racial and Gender Report Card: National Basketball Association."

15. Lapchick, "The 2017 Racial and Gender Report Card: National Football League."

16. Lapchick, "The 2018 Racial and Gender Report Card: National Basketball Association."

17. Richard Lapchick. "Collegiate Athletic Leadership Still Dominated by White Men: Assessing Diversity among Campus and Conference Leaders for Football Bowl Subdivision (FBS) Schools in the 2016–17 Academic Year." *Institute for Diversity and Ethics in Sport*, 21 Nov. 2016. tidesport.org. Accessed 13 Sept. 2018.

18. "The Pledge and Commitment to Promoting Diversity and Gender Equity in Intercollegiate Athletics." *NCAA*, 18 July 2018. ncaa.org. Accessed 13 Sept. 2018.

19. Marc J. Spears. "The Distressing Lack of Black Leadership in the NBA." *Undefeated*, 1 June 2016. theundefeated.com. Accessed 13 Sept. 2018.

CHAPTER 8. INTEGRATING LEAGUE MANAGEMENT AND PLAYERS' UNIONS

1. Jeanine Ramirez. "NBA's Deputy Commissioner Hasn't Forgotten His Brooklyn Roots." *Spectrum News*, 6 July 2017. spectrumlocalnews.com. Accessed 13 Sept. 2018.

2. Richard Lapchick. "The 2018 Racial and Gender Report Card: National Basketball Association." *Institute for Diversity and Ethics in Sport*, 26 June 2018. tidesport.org. Accessed 13 Sept. 2018.

3. Richard Lapchick. "The 2017 Racial and Gender Report Card: National Football League." *Institute for Diversity and Ethics in Sport*, 18 Oct. 2017. tidesport.org. Accessed 18 June 2018.

4. Richard Lapchick. "The 2018 Racial and Gender Report Card: Major League Baseball." *Institute for Diversity and Ethics in Sport*, 12 Apr. 2018. tidesport.org. Accessed 18 June 2018.

5. "Major League Umpire Roster." *MLB.com*, March 2018. mlb.com. Accessed 13 Sept. 2018.

6. Scott Allen. "MLB's First Black Umpire Broke the Color Barrier on Opening Day in D.C. 50 Years Ago." *Washington Post*, 11 Apr. 2016. washingtonpost.com. Accessed 13 Sept. 2018.

7. Christopher A. Parsons, et al. "Strike Three: Discrimination, Incentives, and Evaluation." *American Economic Review*, vol. 101, no. 4, June 2011.

8. Jeff Hamrick and John Rasp. "The Connection Between Race and Called Strikes and Balls." *Journal of Sports Economics*, vol. 16, no. 7, October 2015.

9. Christopher Ingraham. "What the NBA Can Teach Us about Eliminating Racial Bias." *Washington Post*, 25 Feb. 2014. washingtonpost.com. Accessed 9 July 2018.

10. Richard Lapchick. "The 2017 Women's National Basketball Association Racial and Gender Report Card." *Institute for Diversity and Ethics in Sport*, 15 Nov. 2017. tidesport.org. Accessed 9 July 2018.

11. Richard Lapchick. "The WNBA Leads All Leagues in Diversity and Inclusion." *ESPN*, 16 Nov. 2017. espn.com. Accessed 30 June 2018.

CHAPTER 9. FIGHTING THE STEREOTYPES

1. Ahiza Garcia. "These Are the Only Two Owners of Color in the NFL." *CNN Money*, 18 May 2018. money.cnn.com. Accessed 19 July 2018.

2. Mark J. Spears. "The NBA's Leaders Open Up about the League's Diversity Problem." *Undefeated*, 6 June 2016. theundefeated.com. Accessed 9 July 2018.

3. Spears, "The NBA's Leaders Open Up about the League's Diversity Problem."

4. Derrek Asberry. "Pro Baseball Minority Manager Hires Lag Behind Diversity on the Field." *Post and Courier*, 26 May 2018. postandcourier.com. Accessed 10 July 2018.

5. Asberry, "Pro Baseball Minority Manager Hires Lag Behind Diversity on the Field."

INDEX

ABOUT THE AUTHORS

DUCHESS HARRIS, JD, PHD

Professor Harris is the chair of the American Studies department at Macalester College and curator of the Duchess Harris Collection of ABDO books. She is the author and coauthor of recently released ABDO books including *Hidden Human Computers: The Black Women of NASA*, *Black Lives Matter*, and *Race and Policing*.

Before working with ABDO, she authored several other books on the topics of race, culture, and American history. She served as an associate editor for *Litigation News*, the American Bar Association Section of Litigation's quarterly flagship publication, and was the first editor in chief of *Law Raza*, an interactive online journal covering race and the law, published at William Mitchell College of Law. She has earned a PhD in American Studies from the University of Minnesota and a JD from William Mitchell College of Law.

MICHAEL MILLER

Michael Miller is a prolific and best-selling writer. He has written more than 200 nonfiction books for both adult and young readers on a variety of topics, including technology, music, and business. He is known for his ability to explain a wide variety of complex topics to an everyday audience. Collectively, his books have sold more than 1.5 million copies worldwide. In addition to writing books and articles, Miller is also a consultant, speaker, and drummer. He lives with his wife, several stepchildren, and six grandchildren in the Twin Cities area of Minnesota.